Original title:
Life: A Comedy of Errors

Copyright © 2025 Creative Arts Management OÜ
All rights reserved.

Author: Sebastian Whitmore
ISBN HARDBACK: 978-1-80566-151-1
ISBN PAPERBACK: 978-1-80566-446-8

Whirl of Witty Misfortune

In a dance of slips and trips,
We stumble through silly flips.
With laughter masking every fall,
We waltz through chaos, having a ball.

A sandwich lands upon my shoe,
My coffee spills—oh what a view!
Yet every blunder brings a cheer,
As friends all gather round, my dear.

A Mirthful Mosaic

Through the jumbled paths we roam,
Each misstep leads us further home.
A cat that leaps, a dog that stumbles,
Life's funny twists, how it fumbles!

With socks that clash and hats askew,
We laugh until we're bright as dew.
A quirky tale in every face,
We find the joy in every place.

The Fumble Fiesta

A fork that flies, a plate that bounces,
Every meal, the laughter flounces.
When butter slips aside my toast,
We can't help but giggle the most.

A stumble here, a tumble there,
Each clumsy act, a breath of air.
With every blunder, we unite,
Celebrate the jests of our plight.

Turned About and Tickled

In the circus of daily grind,
We juggle woes, a laugh we find.
A twist, a turn, the world goes round,
We chuckle at the upside down.

When plans go south, we take a cue,
To flip the script and start anew.
With every hiccup, joy's the prize,
Together we dance 'neath hilarious skies.

Follies Under the Stars

Under the moon, a cat on a roof,
Danced with a mouse, oh what a goof!
They tumbled and rolled, a sight to behold,
As laughter erupted, the night turned to gold.

A hat on a head, too big for the chap,
He wobbled and tripped, fell flat with a slap!
The stars winked above, in fits of delight,
While he picked up his pride, and took to the night.

The Delicate Dance of Misadventure

Two left feet on a wooden floor,
The tango of chaos, oh what a score!
With missteps galore, and giggles to share,
They spun and they hopped, with clumsy flair.

A pie in the face, a slip on a peel,
The crowd roared with laughter, the joy was unreal.
Even the cat tried to join in the fun,
As pies flew around, and the dance was undone.

The Joy in the Juggle

Three balls in the air, and one in the way,
A juggler named Jim had a wild display.
He fumbled and dropped, with flair and with spin,
The audience cheered, amidst giggles and grins.

With laughter like music, he tried once again,
This time he caught two, oh what a win!
But then comes a dog, with eyes full of cheer,
And swiped the last ball, oh dear, oh dear!

Humorous Hiccups of the Heart

A lover's sweet sigh, turned into a squeak,
A hiccup so loud, it made others peek.
With each tender word, a chuckle arose,
As blushes and laughter mixed in sweet prose.

At dinner for two, spaghetti awry,
With sauce on his shirt and an enchanting lie,
"I'm just saving this for later," he jested,
While she rolled her eyes, her heart so invested.

Giggling at the Gaffes

Fell on a banana peel,
Laughter echoed all around,
Tripped on a tiny heel,
Found my way to the ground.

Mistook my cat for a hat,
Wore it proud until I knew,
That fuzzy feline spat,
And my pride just flew askew.

Spilled coffee on my shirt,
Thought I'd charm the meeting's tide,
Instead, I wore dessert,
And became the joke with pride.

A laugh at every blunder,
Every twist brings joy anew,
In each stumble, a wonder,
Giggles are the world's debut.

Roadblocks and Revelations

Took a wrong turn on a road,
Said hello to a countryside cow,
Found myself in a comedic load,
As it stared with a raised brow.

Lost my keys in the fridge,
Thought I'd find them with ease,
Instead, I flipped through a smidge,
Of pickles, mustard, and peas.

Tripped on my own two feet,
While trying to impress a friend,
Danced right into defeat,
But the giggles would not end.

Every hiccup leads to cheer,
In each stumble, wisdom's gift,
Embrace the folly, my dear,
As we laugh our way adrift.

A Calamity of Merriment

Burnt the dinner to a crisp,
Smoked out the kitchen with flair,
A feast that no one would risk,
Still, we laughed without a care.

Socks that never find their pair,
Searching the nooks of the house,
Chasing gray mice through the air,
But, wait—was that a real mouse?

A mix-up with the laundry,
Whites became a shade of pink,
Fashion statements quite uncanny,
Showing off a cheerful wink.

In every error, delight,
Comedy woven in our days,
Embrace the goofy plight,
And we'll keep laughing always.

The Golden Glimpses of Errors

Wore my shirt inside out,
Didn't notice till the noon,
Strutting proud, without a doubt,
A walking fashion cartoon.

Said the wrong name on a date,
A baffled look crossed their face,
Grinned, I said, 'Isn't it fate?'
Laughter lit up the whole place.

Left my umbrella in the train,
It rained cats and dogs outside,
Drenched but dancing in the rain,
Joyous in the whimsy ride.

In jumbles, we find our grace,
Golden glimmers everywhere,
Embrace each quirky trace,
Laughter lifts us—light as air.

The Comedy of Crumpled Plans

Plans are drawn with careful care,
Yet fate unfolds in wild despair.
A map of hopes, all set to roam,
But every route leads back to home.

With paper crinkles and inkd spots,
We chase the dreams that tie us in knots.
A treasure hunt for things misplaced,
Oh, how we laugh as we are chased!

When socks get lost, the jar won't seal,
A sandwich made, with dubious meal.
The punchline lands, oh what a sight,
The circus of our daily plight.

In tangled webs of joy and jest,
We trip and tumble, but we're blessed.
For every folly, every fall,
Is just a joke we tell to all.

Smiles in the Shadows of Blunders

In shadows cast by little fumbles,
We find the giggles, we find the grumbles.
A shoe untied, a misread sign,
We dance through errors, all is fine.

Coffee spills and papers fly,
An oven's beep, the cat's sly pry.
Each silly slip, a comic twist,
In laughter's clutch, we can't resist.

Lost keys tucked in the fridge's chill,
Mistakes like these give us a thrill.
We face our foes with playful pride,
Among the blunders, joy won't hide.

Embrace the chaos, make it your song,
With every misstep, we grow more strong.
For life's a stage of funny plays,
In blunders' glow, we find our rays.

Whirlwind of Whims

A breeze of thoughts, they swirl and twirl,
With whims that laugh and giggle and whirl.
A recipe tossed with too much spice,
 The kitchen turns into a dice.

Unexpected guests and cakes unmade,
A game of charades where we misplayed.
Juggling dreams on a paper plate,
 Our hearts alight, we laugh at fate.

Socks mismatched in a vibrant glow,
A tangled dance, a rowdy show.
With every thought that doesn't land,
 We spin in circles, hand in hand.

In fanciful chaos, we find delight,
A circus ride, a comical fight.
So let the winds of whimsy blow,
 And turn our lives into a show.

Sip of Silliness

A sip of joy from cup of cheer,
With giggles shared amongst us here.
Spilling tea on our favorite book,
We find the fun in every nook.

With every swig, a chuckle bursts,
Over toast that sadly lacks the crusts.
A splash of cream, a wobble bright,
In silly scenes, we find our light.

Dancing spoons and playful grins,
Whispers soft, where laughter begins.
A fruity punch, with fizz and flair,
Every sip, a breath of air!

So raise your cups to gaffes unplanned,
With silly spirits, hand in hand.
For life served sweet, with frothy fun,
Is best enjoyed when shared by one.

Laughter Among the Blunders

In a world that spins with chance,
Mistakes lead us to dance.
We trip on our own feet,
Yet find joy in the heat.

A coffee spill on a fresh shirt,
Turns out to be quite the flirt.
A laugh echoes through the air,
As we stumble without a care.

Jokes are made at our expense,
Yet we bask in the pretense.
With every trip, a new tale,
In this spectacle, we sail.

So let's raise a toast to the goofs,
Where laughter yields the best proofs.
For in these blunders we find cheer,
A funny story to share, my dear.

Missteps in the Moonlight

Under the glow of the silver rays,
We dance in our own quirky ways.
With two left feet, we spin around,
Finding humor in every sound.

The night is filled with silly falls,
With laughter ringing through the halls.
As stars twinkle and wink above,
We trip and laugh, that's our love.

A forgotten line, a slipped-up cue,
Yet smiles unfold, bright and true.
In every blunder, we are free,
Finding grace in the clumsiness, you see.

So hold my hand, and let us sway,
Through this chaos, we'll find our way.
For under the moon's gentle light,
Our missteps turn to pure delight.

The Clumsy Dance of Existence

With each step, a graceful spill,
Life's a comic, brightened thrill.
We may stumble, we may fall,
Yet laughter is the best of all.

A tumble down the stairs so grand,
Turns into a joke well planned.
We juggle dreams with no finesse,
Joy thrives in our funny mess.

A wrong turn on a winding road,
Brings us tales that can't erode.
We chuckle at the paths we stray,
In our clumsy dance, we play.

With every misstep, we grow bold,
In this saga, we find our gold.
So let's rejoice in the absurd,
For joy in clumsiness is preferred.

Tales of the Unintended

In a world where plans may sway,
We find joy in the disarray.
Intentions may be pure and bright,
But outcomes play a different light.

A pie baked, yet burned to a crisp,
Turns into laughter with every wisp.
We share our tales of what went wrong,
Turning mishaps into a song.

From tangled cords to missed trains,
Comedy blooms in our small pains.
With a wink, we march ahead,
In this circus, we've been led.

So take my hand, let's twirl and weave,
In these tales, we do believe.
For unintended paths are sweet,
With laughter as our heartbeat.

When Fate Trips on Its Feet

The cat on the roof, it jumps with flair,
But lands in a puddle, oh what a scare!
We dress for a meeting, all smart and neat,
Yet step in the mud, our shoes can't compete.

A cake for the party, we baked with glee,
But forgot the sugar, so bitter, you see!
We laugh at the fumbles, the slips and falls,
In this waltz with fate, we stand tall through it all.

Chaos in the Routine

The clock yells at us, 'It's time for a run!'
But we trip on the laces, oh isn't this fun?
A coffee spill here, the toast on the floor,
Our morning parade feels like a circus galore.

The grocery list speaks, but we buy what's wrong,
Forget the essentials, our cart's singing a song!
We chuckle and smile at the mess we've amassed,
In this sitcom of chaos, we're having a blast.

The Tapestry of Misfortune

A thread pulls here, a stitch goes astray,
Our plans unravel, but hey, that's okay!
With each drop of ink, the canvas gets wild,
For what's drawn with laughter is forever beguiled.

The misdirection sings, and we dance in the mist,
A plot twist appears, how could we resist?
With brushes of folly, we color the scene,
Life's greatest mishaps are often the mean.

Laugh Lines and Lessons

A wrinkle of wisdom, a tale in each fold,
In the book of blunders, we're daring and bold.
We gather our stories, a comical crew,
Each laugh shared today will guide us anew.

With smiles for the slip-ups and cheers for the fall,
We find joy in chaos, it's the best laugh of all.
For each blunder witnessed, a lesson does bloom,
As we dance through the errors, our hearts find their room.

The Clown's Dilemma

With oversized shoes and red nose,
He trips on the rug as everyone knows.
A pie in the face, a slapstick surprise,
Laughter erupts as he fumbles and cries.

Balloon animals twist and twist,
But they pop in his hands, it's too hard to resist.
Slipping on marbles, he spins like a top,
In the circus of chaos, he never can stop.

Juggling with oranges, they fly in the air,
One bounces away, but he doesn't care.
A tumble, a roll, he laughs all the way,
In the jest of his world, he savors the play.

Under the spotlight, he takes a grand bow,
The heart of the show, he makes it somehow.
For even in fails, there's joy to be found,
In the dance of the foolish, love's laughter resounds.

Hiccups in the Harmony

A lullaby played, yet hiccups arise,
Each note interrupted, a comedic surprise.
Singing so sweet, then a snort breaks the tune,
Harmony shatters, like a balloon in the afternoon.

The dog join in, with a bark and a howl,
A family serenade turns into a growl.
The baby joins in with a giggle and squeal,
As timing gets lost, who knows how to feel?

A dance in the kitchen turns into a mess,
With spinning and twirling, a haphazard dress.
Feet in a tangle, laughter fills the air,
As hiccups and harmony croon without care.

Back to the chaos, the melody sways,
Through bumps and missteps, the heart still plays.
In a world full of laughter, we all find our part,
With hiccups in harmony, we're never apart.

Bumbles and Blunders

He sets out for coffee, in a hurry and fuss,
Trips on his shoelace, oh what a plus!
Spills on his shirt, now a brown coffee stain,
Wipes it on his pants, oh what a gain!

A pick-me-up ordered, but it's tea instead,
A sip and a cringe, he wishes for bread.
Calls it a day, but forgets his bag,
Strides out the door, feeling quite the hag.

Conversations get tangled, words twist and shout,
"Did I just say that?" he wonders aloud.
With giggles and snorts, the blunders abound,
In the dance of errors, joy can be found.

But with each little fumble, a lesson is told,
That laughter's the gold, and it's worth more than gold.
To shimmy through bumbles with humor in tow,
Is the secret to living, as we stumble and grow.

The Unscripted Script

An actor rehearses, a script in his hand,
But the lines all escape him, it's just not as planned.
With heroes and villains, he fumbles each turn,
In a dramatic twist, it's the laughs that he earns.

The stage is a mess, with props all awry,
A sword made of foam, and a rubber chicken flies.
The audience giggles as they watch in delight,
As he stumbles and bumbles, all through the night.

A cue that he misses brings chaos to play,
What was meant to be drama is just silliness, hey!
From tragedy to laughter, the plot takes a leap,
In the joy of mistakes, memories we keep.

Drawn into laughter, the lines are all blurred,
In a tale of mishaps, no need for a word.
For every misstep is just part of the fun,
In an unscripted script, the laughter's just begun.

The Fabric of Follies

In a world full of slips and slides,
The jester dances, and the folly hides.
Threads of mishap weave the day,
With laughter stitching every fray.

Each step we take, a stumble waits,
We paint our dreams on mismatched plates.
A tapestry of blunders bright,
Creating joy with each delight.

Whims of Whimsy

A hat too big, a shoe too small,
The punchlines echo, we start to fall.
With every twist, a giggling jest,
In this merry chaos, we feel our best.

The toaster burns, the dog runs wild,
In this comedy, we're all but a child.
Whims of whimsy paint the sky,
Beneath the laughter, we learn to fly.

A Fool's Footnote in Time

With rhymes that trip and puns that tangle,
A fool's bright footnote, ready to dangle.
In the margins of reason, we scribble our glee,
Capturing moments, oh, joyously free.

What's planned is undone in a wink,
We laugh at the chaos, make time rethink.
Footnotes glow with stories untold,
A comedy of joy, more precious than gold.

Laughter Beneath a Veil of Mistakes

Behind closed doors, the mishaps bloom,
Curious tales that dispel the gloom.
A trip on a laugh, a tumble of cheer,
With every blunder, we hold it dear.

In every error, a spark ignites,
We gather the joy, like firefly lights.
Beneath the veil where slips abide,
Laughter rules and pitfalls slide.

The Mirthful Maze

In a world of twists and turns,
We stumble through each day,
With laughter in our hearts,
We trip along the way.

Step on a banana peel,
Fall flat on our face,
We roll with the giggles,
And dance in the disgrace.

Coffee spills upon our shirt,
A toast that went awry,
We toast to our blunders,
As we watch our drinks fly.

Through every crooked path,
We cheerfully embrace,
For in this joyful mess,
We find our happy place.

A Joyride of Misjudgments

With each lift of the wheel,
We swerve a little wide,
Turn right when we should left,
And crash with careless pride.

The GPS is lost again,
Recalculating our fate,
But who needs a map when,
Adventure waits in spate?

Singing off-key in the car,
What's wrong with this tune?
A hiccup leads to laughter,
As we chase the silly moon.

Stopping at the wrong café,
For toast and cold, strange soup,
We'll feast on smiling errors,
Join our happy troop.

Catastrophes in Color

Woke up in polka dots,
Uneven shoes askew,
We paint the day in laughter,
With every silly hue.

Spilled paint upon the floor,
An artist in dismay,
Our masterpiece of mishaps,
Turns chaos into play.

The pink turned into orange,
And violet into green,
A rainbow of blunders,
That's truly unforeseen.

With problems painted brightly,
We smile through the show,
In the gallery of life,
Who cares which way we go?

Gleeful Gaffes

With every clumsy moment,
We giggle through the day,
A misstep here, a stumble,
Our worries tossed away.

Forgotten names and faces,
Each grin a borrowed smile,
We slip on jokes and puns,
To make our day worthwhile.

A wardrobe malfunction,
The buttons all askew,
Embracing the ridiculous,
With every silly view.

For in this clumsy dance,
We find the joy we seek,
And from our gleeful gaffes,
Our laughter starts to peak.

A Fool's Quest for Normalcy

In search of normal, I wear mismatched socks,
Stumbling through days like a box of old clocks.
I tripped over dreams, they scattered like crumbs,
Yet laughter escapes as my folly becomes.

I fumble with choices, like keys that don't fit,
Pretending I know what I'm doing a bit.
Yet life's little quirks paint smiles on my face,
For tripping on whims is my favorite race.

With quirks in my pocket and joy in the air,
I dance through the chaos, without any care.
Each tumble a treasure, each blunder a gift,
In the madness of normal, I find my own lift.

So here's to the jester, the fool on this spree,
Who chases the ordinary yet stays wild and free.
In the land of the curious, I laugh and I twirl,
For the art of the silly is my kind of world.

Serendipity's Slipshod Steps.

I slipped on a breeze as I walked through the park,
Met a dog who could dance, and we soared like a lark.
With tangled up shoelaces, I tried to look cool,
But tripped on a squirrel, oh, nature's own fool!

The sunset was messy, all oranges and blues,
While I spilled my drink on my favorite shoes.
Each twist and each turn, a new question arose,
Why not laugh at the chaos, when nothing quite flows?

Like bumping into shadows on a moonlit night,
I chuckle at stumbles that rarely feel right.
Though plans may unravel and wiggle away,
It's the giggles that follow that brighten my day.

So here's to the blunders, the mishaps, the glee,
To the perfectly wrong paths that lead us to spree.
In this dance of confusion, I twirl and take part,
For fortune favors the slipshod heart.

Whimsical Whispers of the Heart

Oh, whispers of wonder, they tickle my ear,
As the world spins around in a grand cavalier.
I wore a top hat to dinner, quite bold, you might say,
While my soup spoon became a banjo today!

I followed a rabbit right down a dark hole,
Found a party of mice, each sharing a roll.
With tea made of laughter and cookies so bright,
We toasted to nonsense under the moonlight.

Each tickle of whimsy ignites sparks of delight,
I twirl with my shadows while losing my might.
In this circus of moments, I stumble and cheer,
For spontaneity's magic is better than fear.

So listen to whispers, let giggles unfold,
For joy hides in oddness, a treasure to hold.
As I dance with the strange and embrace all the quirks,
In the heart of the whirl, my spirit just lurks.

The Jester's Truths

A jester in disguise, with a grin ear to ear,
I juggle my thoughts, turning folly to cheer.
With a hat full of puns and a heart full of grace,
I find wisdom in laughter, no serious face.

I spilled coffee today, made a wonderful mess,
The world's not so serious, despite human stress.
With chuckles like confetti, I dance through the day,
Turning sorrow to giggles, come what may.

Each stumble's a story, each fool's laugh a song,
I embrace all the oddities, where I belong.
With a wink and a twist, my truth takes its flight,
In the light of the silly, my heart shines so bright.

So come one, come all, to this whimsical show,
Where we laugh at the blunders, and let the joy flow.
In the court of the jester, we're free to be us,
For the jest of existence is simply a plus.

Bumbling Through the Pages of Time

I tripped on my shoelace, fell into a dream,
A monkey in a tux, playing in a stream.
The clock laughed at me, its hands in a whirl,
While I scrambled to dance with a dizzying twirl.

My cat wore a hat, he looked quite refined,
As I spilled my tea, just to see what I'd find.
A turtle with glasses scribbled notes fast,
While I chased my own tail, a whirlwind of past.

A mishap at dinner—oh, what a delight!
I served up my noodles with socks on the side.
Each bite brought a chuckle; dessert was a farce,
A pie full of rubber bands, oh, how we'd laugh!

So here's to the blunders, to laughter as glue,
In the book of my life, I'm the jester—it's true.
With each turned page, I find humor divine,
In the clumsy ballet of moments benign.

The Unscripted Nature of Joy

I waltzed in the rain with my mismatched shoes,
While birds chirped my theme song, I danced with the blues.
The sun popped his head from behind a gray cloud,
And I slipped on a banana, so loud!

In a world full of scripts, I stumbled and tripped,
Whispers of laughter as I awkwardly quipped.
A goat in a bowtie inspected my fence,
As I tried to explain just what was my sense.

The ice cream was melting, my heart reached the peak,
A cone full of sprinkles was all I could seek.
But the scoop slipped right off, bounced and rolled down,

As I chased after joy, in a colorful gown.

In this crazy charade, I embrace every fall,
With each twist and turn, I'm having a ball.
For who needs a script when the heart holds the key,
To the unscripted giggles that set our souls free?

Laughter's Lament

Oh, the cake was a flop, and the candles too bright,
It toppled and tumbled, a comical sight.
We clapped way too loud as it splashed on the floor,
And laughter erupted, we begged for some more!

The socks were a treasure, mismatched and bold,
Danced on the table, like stories retold.
Each twist in our path was a chuckle to share,
While we juggled our hopes in the cool evening air.

My phone took a dive in the punch bowl's embrace,
It blared out a song with an impeccable grace.
We sang out of tune, yet in harmony swayed,
As the moments grew richer, our worries betrayed.

Here's to laughter's lament, so catchy and bright,
As we whirl through the chaos, our hearts taking flight.
In this circus of blunders, we find our delight,
With a wink and a grin, we dance through the night.

Haphazardly Hitched Hopes

With a suitcase of dreams and wheels that squeak,
I set off to conquer a world that's unique.
But the road signs all giggled, and tricks played out,
As I lost my way, filled with hope yet in doubt.

My compass spun wildly; it pointed to fun,
Each detour a treasure, for battles I've won.
I met dancing frogs on a very straight path,
Who showed me the art of whimsical math.

The train I had boarded was covered in paint,
With a rooster as conductor, quite far from quaint.
I missed my stop laughing at the sight so absurd,
Yet joy is the journey, and not just the word.

So I'll wander these routes, with heart in my hands,
Through whimsical places and magical lands.
For haphazardly hitched hopes take flight without care,
As I revel in mishaps, each moment to share.

Echoes of Happy Accidents

Stumbled on a banana peel, oh what a sight,
Laughter erupts as I tumble, delight!
A dog fetches my dignity, runs out the gate,
With each fall, I learn to embrace my fate.

Overcooked pasta turns into a gooey ball,
My chef skills vanish, oh how they fall!
Dinner guests laugh, it's a quirky feast,
In blunders like these, joy is released.

A coffee spill paints my shirt like art,
Fashion faux pas, but that's just the start!
With every mishap, a story is spun,
Echoes of laughter, we're all just having fun.

Who knew that tripping could bring such glee?
In each stumble, a spark of comedy.
So let's toast to the laughs, both big and small,
In the grand parade of mistakes, we're having a ball!

The Smile Behind the Slip

I stepped on a toy, oh how I soared,
Through the air like a bird, suddenly floored!
But as I landed in the plush living room,
Laughter erupted, dispelling my gloom.

Chasing my cat, I outpaced my own shoes,
Down went my pride as I fell with a snooze.
Amidst the chaos, a giggle slipped through,
For every misstep, a comedy cue.

My recipe called for zest, I grabbed the salt,
Dinner went south, but who'd blame my default?
With every bite, faces twist in surprise,
Yet joy swims deep behind all the cries.

Slipping on ice was a dance of delight,
Spinning and laughing, all wrongs turned to right.
In each little fall, a grand story hides,
With smiles so bright, how sweetly life guides.

Chasing Shadows of What Might Have Been

I wore mismatched socks to a formal affair,
People did stare, but I just didn't care.
Each cheeky glance held a giggle so bright,
In fashion mistakes, there's pure delight.

On the way to the party, I took a wrong turn,
Found a great cafe where my spirits did yearn.
A detour of laughter, I sipped and I cheered,
In the heart of mishaps, joy reappeared.

Emails sent wrong that had folks in stitches,
A reply of confusion, oh aren't we all witches?
Chasing these shadows, I find my true way,
Through twists and turns, laughter's here to stay.

So here's to the moments when plans go astray,
In the jumbles of life, we'll find humor's play.
With every misstep and every wrong cue,
We'll cherish the blunders, and giggle anew!

Hiccups in the Harmony

The song skipped a beat at the karaoke night,
My voice cracked and wobbled, quite a funny sight.
But in that odd moment, we all burst in cheer,
It's hiccups in harmony that we hold dear.

Balancing drinks while dancing a jig,
The splash on my friend made the whole place dig!
With giggles contagious, we tapped our toes,
In silly blunders, true joy often grows.

A joke gone wrong turned into a play,
With twists and turns that led us astray.
We laughed till we cried, in moments absurd,
In hiccups of harmony, joy is interred.

So let's embrace each awkward little scene,
For in these funny slips, happiness gleans.
With laughter as our soundtrack, let's join the dance,
Through life's little hiccups, here's to our chance!

Governance of Giggles

In a world of slips and slides,
The rulers trip in grand parades.
With papers flying, laughter hides,
They juggle woes like circus aids.

Plans are drawn on napkin sheets,
While coffee spills on eager notes.
They fumble votes with clumsy feats,
And dance like ducks on tiny boats.

Oh, what fun to steer the ship,
While waving at the sea of fools.
With every bob and every blip,
Each blunder's turned to golden jewels.

So raise a glass to all the jesters,
Who draft the laws while spilling wine.
With every laughter, may we pester,
The governance of giggles divine.

A Serenade of Stumbles

In a garden where the daisies wink,
A serenade of trips takes flight.
With every step, a quick rethink,
As falling blooms provide delight.

The cat sings tunes while chasing tails,
A melody of misfit paws.
While laughter dances, joy prevails,
And falls become poetic flaws.

Beneath the sun, the shadows chase,
The attempters of the dance routine.
In every tumble, a smiling face,
We waltz through scenes both brave and keen.

With every slip, a song grows loud,
A symphony of gleeful flops.
Let's serenade the silly crowd,
Where stumbles live and laughter hops.

When Clowns Brush the Canvas

In a world where colors bleed,
Clowns paint smiles on heavy hearts.
With every stroke, they plant a seed,
   Of laughter woven into arts.

They stumble over cans of paint,
While juggling dreams with clownish grace.
They splash the walls with colors quaint,
   As hiccups draw a giggling face.

With bows and wigs, they take the stage,
   Their antics bend the lines of fate.
   As laughter fills the bustling page,
   An art of joy we celebrate.

So let the clowns with brushes sway,
   Creating chaos, bright and bold.
   In every hue, they find a way,
   To turn our frowns to tales retold.

Laughter on the Wrong Side of the Tracks

On tracks where train of thought derails,
With whistles blowing, sounds of glee.
The passengers tell silly tales,
Of mishaps on this comical spree.

They miss the stops with carefree smiles,
As wheels skip over bumps and gaps.
With every turn, it's far from miles,
And laughter fills the noisy laps.

From windows wide, the world's a jest,
Where chaos reigns and fun prevails.
Each wrong route proves to be the best,
As joy rides high on silly rails.

So take a ride on wobbly tracks,
And join a crew that swims in laughs.
For every twist, our humor racks—
Laughter blooms in all our gaffs.

The Art of Fumbling Grace

With every step, a stumble made,
A dance of clumsiness displayed.
We juggle dreams like spinning plates,
And laugh at all our happy fates.

A misstep here, a slip away,
We trip through life, come what may.
Our balance shifts, our shirts do cling,
Yet find the joy in every fling.

The world's our stage, so vast and wide,
We fumble forth, with hearts our guide.
Each pratfall's gift, a lesson shared,
In comic tears, we're all ensnared.

Embrace the flaws, the bumbles spin,
For in the mess, the fun begins.
With laughter loud and spirits bright,
We waltz through blunders, pure delight.

Serendipity's Script

A script unwritten, lines askew,
We dance on stage, just me and you.
With every plot twist, eyes grow wide,
As life's surprise becomes our guide.

A coffee spill, a chance encounter,
We find the joy, through every flounder.
The universe chuckles, nudges slow,
With playful whispers, 'Just let go.'

Mistaken texts and funny faces,
We wander through the oddest places.
Destined paths, yet off we stray,
Creating laughs, come what may.

In every mishap, something's gleamed,
A treasure found, an errant dream.
So take a bow, embrace the jest,
For this wacky twist is our best.

The Playful Tumble of Time

With clock hands spinning, time takes flight,
We chase the minutes, day and night.
A tumble here, a giggle there,
We play the fool without a care.

Time fumbles forth, a jester bold,
We age like wine, or so we're told.
Each wrinkle tells a tale so grand,
In the circus of life, we take a stand.

We drop our goals like clumsy fools,
Yet embrace the chaos, break the rules.
For in this game of chasing fate,
We find the joy in being late.

Laugh at the clock, it spins so fast,
In playful moments, memories cast.
With every slip, our hearts will chime,
In the merriment of fleeting time.

Folly's Footprints on the Path

Step by step, we tread along,
With folly's song, we can't go wrong.
Each footprint leaves a tale behind,
Of silly moments, sweetly blind.

We dance on puddles, trip on stones,
And chuckle at our silly moans.
The path is wild, with twists and turns,
In playful folly, our spirit yearns.

Navigating through the ups and downs,
We laugh with friends and share our frowns.
For every bump, a lesson found,
In delightful absurdity, we're wound.

So cheer to folly, our faithful guide,
In this madcap journey, let's glide.
With laughter bright, we'll pave the way,
On folly's path, we'll always play.

A Bouquet of Blunders

In a garden of missteps, blooms seem so bright,
A flower of folly takes its flight.
With petals of laughter, and stems of surprise,
We gather our giggles, under sunny skies.

The bee trips and tumbles, a dance on the breeze,
As daisies chuckle, with utmost ease.
The gardener fumbles, his seeds go astray,
Yet petals of humor still flower today.

With each sprout of chaos, the colors rejoice,
In this patch of silliness, hear the loud voice.
For in this bouquet, mistakes multiply,
In the scheme of the garden, who dares ask why?

So gather your giggles, adorn your attire,
In this comedic garden, your heart will aspire.
Each blunder a blossom, each chuckle a bloom,
Together we flourish, dispelling all gloom.

The Jester's Journey

A jester sets off, with bells on his shoes,
He trips on a log, spreads laughter and ooze.
With a wink and a grin, he juggles his fate,
Each fumble a step in his dance with the great.

He visits a town where the folks are all bright,
But he slips on a peel, what a comical sight!
With laughter erupting, the crowd starts to cheer,
For foolish missteps are the jokes they hold dear.

Through valleys of blunders, he dances with glee,
Each misadventure brings joy as the key.
A laugh is a treasure, he hoards like a king,
In the realm of the jesters, he'll always take wing.

So join in the fun, let your worries outplay,
In this journey of jokes, let's twirl and sway.
With each twist and tumble, let humor take flight,
For the jester's adventure is sheer pure delight.

Joy in the Jigsaw

A puzzle laid out, pieces random and wild,
Each fit brings a giggle, like a mischievous child.
With edges all jumbled, we laugh at the mess,
Finding joy in the chaos, it's anyone's guess.

The image is blurry; the colors collide,
A duck with a hat, or a boat full of pride?
We fit them together, chuckles fill the air,
In this jigsaw of life, we joyfully dare.

With a twist and a turn, the pieces align,
What started as nonsense becomes quite divine.
Each blunder a treasure, each laugh a delight,
In the joyful assembly, everything feels right.

So gather those fragments, let laughter ignite,
For joy is the puzzle that makes wrongs feel right.
In this tapestry woven with grins and with cheer,
Each piece is a memory, precious and dear.

The Pun of Potential

In a world full of puns, where words like to play,
Where every slip spoken brings smiles to the fray.
The potential is endless, in laughter we find,
That humor is richer with each silly bind.

A baker bakes bread, but the dough takes a dive,
As crumbs flow like laughter, it's how we survive.
With wordplay and blunders, we craft our own fate,
Each pun an adventure, a twist full of fate.

The cat on a mat tries to plot out a purr,
But ends up in chaos, the whiskers all stir.
When potential meets folly, a masterpiece blooms,
In the garden of laughter, all worry just zooms.

So cheer for the mischief, embrace every jest,
For in the world's laughter, we are truly blessed.
As we dance with our quips and our playful intent,
We'll find that potential is where joy is spent.

The Humor of Happenstance

A slip on the floor, who could foresee?
A sandwich goes flying, oh woe is me!
Laughing so hard, tears in my eyes,
Mishaps like these are no great surprise.

Chasing a dog, I trip on a shoe,
He winks at the cat, as if he just knew.
Laughter erupts, as I eat dirt's taste,
In this goofy dance, there's not a moment to waste.

The clock strikes twelve; my hair's a wild mess,
Dressed in pajamas that surely confess.
Yet here I am, ready to cheer,
In the grand play of life, joy is sincere!

So raise a glass to the blunders we make,
Each funny twist brings another awake.
With smiles and giggles, let's set the tone,
In this absurd show, we are never alone.

Antics of an Errant Soul

I tried to shine shoes, but stepped in glue,
Now I'm the one with a sticky shoe too!
With customers laughing, I bow with a grin,
Today's grand failure makes for good din.

Wobbly on skates, I take to the floor,
A pirouette, oh wait! There's the door!
Down with a thump, the crowd roars with glee,
This graceful disaster is just so me.

A soup on my shirt, I wear it with pride,
A true mark of joy, how can I hide?
"Call it a style!" I proudly proclaim,
Where laughter is currency, I've struck gold fame.

In the chaos of moments, I dance and I trip,
Finding delight in each foolish blip.
For every misstep that leads to despair,
Is a chance to chuckle and lighten the air.

The Tragicomedy of Moments

In the middle of dinner, my fork took a flight,
It landed on Grandma, oh what a sight!
Laughter erupted as she jeered with grace,
In this family feast, I just found my place.

A text meant for Janet went to a Joe,
"Love you!" I typed and felt my heart slow.
He replied with a laugh, "Let's date for a while!"
Such a blunder turned into a cheerful smile.

In the rain, I slipped on a fresh puddle,
With flailing arms, I turned it to muddle.
As I splashed and rolled, like a fish without aim,
The world just chuckled at my funny game.

So here's to the mishaps that color our days,
In every blunder, there's wisdom that plays.
With laughter in the air, let's toast to those deeds,
With humor as our guide, we'll fulfill all our needs.

Clumsy Poise in Motion

Walking with swagger, I trip on a rock,
My coolness disrupted, a real shock!
With a tumble and roll, I regain my stance,
Just a part of the show, welcome to the dance!

A sneeze in a meeting, a loud, surprise sound,
The coffee spills forth, oh what a rebound!
Yet in the awkwardness, we all join in glee,
A moment of laughter brings unity.

Chasing the cat, I trip on my shoelace,
Down to the ground with such little grace.
She looks back and laughs, then dashes away,
Teaching me joy is just a paw's play.

So let's toast to errors, those silly old things,
In the mess of our journey, a light laughter sings.
With clumsy poise, we twirl and we sway,
In this circus of moments, we dance and we play.

The Chaotic Canvas of Yesterdays

In a world where clowns paint skies,
Mismatched socks start the surprise.
Bananas slip in the hallway,
Laughter echoes as we sway.

Each blunder, a splash of cheer,
A dance of fate that draws us near.
Juggling dreams with a wink and grin,
Crafting joy, though it may spin.

And when we trip, we skip with glee,
The universe laughs back at me.
With every fall, a story told,
We wear our mishaps bright and bold.

Brush strokes wild, we paint our tale,
Chasing sunlight through the hail.
Each error, a color, a vibrant hue,
Together we create, just me and you.

Euphoria in Every Oops

Oops, I spilled my drink again,
A fountain burst from careless zen.
Socks don't match, but who's to care?
We laugh and dance without a spare.

Caught in traffic, lost in thought,
The GPS has truly fought.
A wrong turn leads to pizza's joy,
Serendipity's sweet ploy.

Tripping over words we say,
Make each moment bright as day.
In every mishap, joy will bloom,
Euphoria fills every room.

So let's embrace this silly ride,
With giggles as our trusted guide.
For every slip a lesson learned,
In the dance of life, we're unconcerned.

The Satire of Serendipity

A hat on head, but shoes awry,
I wave to clouds that laugh and sigh.
Each twist of fate a funny jest,
In chaos, I find my best.

Spilled ink turns into a swan,
A daydream slipped, but onward drawn.
Accidental art, a genius flair,
Life's little quirks, a wild affair.

Stumbles become a dashing feat,
We laugh together, feel the beat.
With open hearts, the world aligns,
In every error, joy entwines.

So raise your glass to splendid flops,
To every curve our folly drops.
In this grand play, we're all the stars,
With every goof, we shine like cars.

Errors Painted in Pastel

A canvas bright with pastel hues,
Every line a smile, each shade a muse.
A raincoat worn on a sunny day,
We giggle at the way we stray.

In kitchen chaos, pancakes fly,
Maple syrup, oh my, oh my!
Every burnt toast, a crown of grace,
We find delight in every place.

With slippery floors and crazy clocks,
We dance around like silly jocks.
Each scratch and smudge, a work of art,
In mischief's grasp, we take our part.

So here's to joy in every blunder,
Life's playful script, a sweet wonder.
In this gallery of cute defects,
We paint the world with laughter's effects.

A Tapestry of Twists and Turns

In a world where plans go awry,
I trip on my shoelace, oh my!
Maps lead to places not on the chart,
Yet I dance like a fool, with laughter and heart.

Every step I take feels so misled,
But oh, the adventures that fill my head!
I juggle my dreams with a wink and a grin,
Finding joy in the chaos, it's where I begin.

Who knew a flat tire would spark such delight?
The moon carries secrets as I ride through the night.
With friends full of giggles, and tales that grow,
Every twist is a treasure, with more tales to show.

So raise a glass high to the folly we share,
In this wacky journey, we're beyond compare!
It's a vibrant tapestry, full of silly designs,
Each mistake just a thread in these colorful lines.

When Laughter Leads the Way

With every step upon this stage,
I trip on my words, a laugh to gauge.
I flip through the script, oh what a mess,
But the joy in the blunders is truly the best.

The cat steals my sandwich, the dog chews my shoe,
Amidst all the chaos, my laughter grew.
Every coffee spill leads to comical claims,
And the punchline, oh, it always finds names!

Chasing my dreams on a rollercoaster ride,
With a pie in my face, and no place to hide.
Yet with each wild ride, I find pure delight,
As laughter becomes my guiding light.

So here's to the moments where we wildly stray,
When the silliness swings on the light of the day.
For when laughter leads me, I follow with glee,
In this humorous journey, I'm joyful and free.

The Silly Symphony of Mistakes

In the grand symphony of the day,
I step on the beat, what a comedic display!
With violins screeching as I trip on a phone,
The audience giggles, I'm never alone.

Each blunder's a note in this awkward tune,
Fumbling and laughing beneath the bright moon.
With trumpets and laughter ringing through the air,
Every misstep just adds to the flare.

With a conductor's baton made of dreams and wishes,
I lead this wild orchestra, a bowl full of fishes.
As the drums beat loud, I embrace each mistake,
For in this silly symphony, joy's what I make.

So let's dance together, as the music goes on,
For the laughter and giggles are never gone.
In this concert of life, it's the fun that we crave,
Each error a melody—a moment to save!

A Juggling Act of Joy

I juggle my worries with a smile on my face,
As oranges and lemons take up their place.
One slips from my hand, what a silly blunder,
Yet I laugh as it rolls beneath the blue thunder.

Balancing dreams like a circus of clowns,
With socks on my hands, and mismatched gowns.
I stumble and giggle, the crowd is amused,
In a waltz of the goofy, I feel so infused.

Each toss a reminder of the fun in the fall,
Like balloons that float, or a cat in a hall.
With every odd moment that makes my heart sing,
I cherish each giggle that this chaos can bring.

So let the bright colors of joy take their flight,
In this juggling act, everything feels right.
For in every folly, a lesson to learn,
It's the warmth of the laughter that makes my heart burn.

Stumbling Towards Serenity

I tripped on my hopes, fell flat on my face,
The mirror laughed back at my silly embrace.
I chased after wisdom, took a wrong turn,
Now I'm learning to juggle my midnight concern.

Each blunder a dance, a step in the show,
I wear my misfortunes like a bright, silly bow.
With every new tumble, I gather the cheer,
For laughter, my friend, conquers every small fear.

The Farce of Fragile Dreams

I built a grand castle from dreams made of sand,
But the tide washed it out with a wave of its hand.
I chased after visions that danced in the night,
Only to find they were shadows in flight.

With each silly falter, I learn to let go,
Navigating folly like a whimsical show.
The punchline of truth is often absurd,
In this circus of chaos, my heart's never stirred.

Unraveled Threads of Fate

I knitted my plans with the silliest yarn,
But the fabric of fate unraveled with charm.
Each stitch I imagined unraveled in glee,
A tapestry woven of pure mystery.

I laughed at the knots, the tangles they bring,
For every mishap can lead to a fling.
In the comedy of moments, I wink at despair,
For joy can be found in the craziest snare.

Ridiculous Revelations

The signs on the road keep pointing the wrong way,
But I'm riding this rollercoaster every day.
With banners of folly flying high in the breeze,
My compass spins wildly, but my heart feels at ease.

I found wisdom tucked in a jester's bright hat,
Turning fumbles to fortune with every silly spat.
So here's to the blunders that shape who we are,
In this ridiculous tale, we all shine like a star!

When the Unexpected Becomes a Blessing

A spilled coffee on a white shirt,
Turns into laughter, not a flirt.
The meeting's delayed, the boss is late,
We share our stories, it's time to create.

A flat tire on a country road,
Leads to a picnic with food bestowed.
Strangers gather, all woes forgot,
In the unexpected, joy is sought.

Plans go awry, not what we planned,
Yet fate's little tricks often expand.
Out of the chaos, friendships bloom,
In the blunders, we chase away gloom.

So dance through the follies, take your chance,
Find magic in mishaps; join the dance.
For every blunder, there's gift to see,
In the twists of fate, we find glee.

The Dance of the Disadvantaged

Two left feet on the floor so wide,
We stumble, trip, but feel the pride.
Laughter echoes in the crowded space,
As we`ll embrace this merry race.

A broken shoe, a frayed old dress,
Yet we dance on, no time for distress.
The music plays, our spirits rise,
We find our rhythm beneath the skies.

When luck is thin, and plans go south,
We tumble forth, mouths full of mouth.
For every slip that makes us grim,
Becomes a laugh to dance on whim.

In awkward steps, we find our grace,
Through silly moves, we hold our place.
The disadvantaged lead the way,
In every misstep, we laugh, we play.

Whimsy in the Wreckage

The toy train derailed, parts all around,
Yet laughter rings out; joy is found.
With blocks strewn about, a fortress made,
In the wreckage, childhood's unafraid.

Puddles invite leaps, splashes galore,
Each stumble and slip opens a door.
The spilled ice cream? A masterpiece,
On the pavement, our worries cease.

When plans go wrong, hearts take flight,
We find merry moments, pure delight.
Amidst the broken, beauty thrives,
In every mess, the funny survives.

So let's gather the pieces, build anew,
With giggles and grins, we'll see it through.
For in our follies, we can't forget,
The joy that grows from our mishap's debt.

The Upside-Down Delight

Waking up late, brunch now a dance,
We flip the script, seize our chance.
Pajamas still on, we rush with glee,
Who knew chaos could be so free?

A recipe fails, smoke fills the air,
Yet laughter erupts; no need to despair.
With burnt toast we make perfect s'mores,
In our kitchen, sunshine pours.

Life takes a turn, upside down spins,
We twirl with fate, embrace our sins.
Through silly mishaps and merry sounds,
We spin like tops, joy abounds.

So flub every task with flair and style,
In each twist and turn, wear a smile.
For when the world turns upside down,
Laughter's the crown for every clown.

Chronicles of Blunders

I wore mismatched shoes today,
One brown, one bright blue.
People laughed and pointed,
But I just smiled too.

I spilled my coffee on my shirt,
Thought it was the cup!
Instead, I found a donut joke,
Now I'm stuck with a pup.

The bus I needed zoomed right past,
I waved like it was mine.
Instead, I tripped and fell, oh dear,
A perfect slapstick sign!

Every day brings fun anew,
With silly little slips.
So I'll embrace the quirky flaws,
And ride the laughter's dips.

The Misadventures of Everyday

I tried to bake a fancy cake,
Instead made a blob.
Tasted like rubber with a twist,
Thank goodness for the hob!

Misread the map on my big trip,
Ended up in a zoo.
Saw a lion munching on a hat,
I thought it looked brand new.

I tripped upon a garden hose,
And fell right on my face.
Turns out the cat just laughed out loud,
In this wild, funny race.

Each day's another chance to fail,
With laughter as my guide.
I'll keep on dancing through these mishaps,
With joy I cannot hide.

A Dance of Mishaps

I attempted to impress a friend,
With cooking skills I lack.
The smoke alarm rang loud and clear,
I served them take-out snack.

I wore my shirt inside-out,
Didn't notice till noon.
A fashion icon in my mind,
But folks just watched and swooned.

The dog stole my sandwich right away,
While I was in a trance.
Now crumbs are all that's left for me,
In this old game of chance.

In every stumble, every slip,
I find a joyful spark.
This dance of errors leads to smiles,
It lights up every dark.

Echoes of Eccentricity

I bought a plant to cheer me up,
But forgot to water long.
Now it's a crispy, sad old friend,
With memories gone wrong.

I texted "Boss" instead of "Babe",
Got a reply so quick.
Now my workplace jokes abound,
And I just feel so thick.

Today I wore two different socks,
A fashion trend, they say.
People ask, "Was that on purpose?"
With a laugh, I shrug away.

Every blunder brings a giggle,
In this world of oddities.
With every echo of mishap,
I find my quirkiest keys.

A Slapstick Saga

In a world where slips abound,
A dog dashed past, I hit the ground.
My coffee flew, a caffeinated arc,
Laughter bloomed, igniting a spark.

Tripping over my laces too tight,
Caught in a dance, what a silly sight.
The banana peel lurking, oh what a tease,
With every fall, I aim to please.

A pie in the face, a classic delight,
Who knew my cat had such a fight?
Chasing shadows, dodging fate,
Each blunder has me laughing late.

So let's embrace the comic strife,
In every tumble, there's joy in life.
With giggles echoing through the day,
In this wild farce, we laugh and sway.

The Art of Missing the Mark

A dart to the bullseye? What a dream!
Instead, I hit the wall with a gleam.
Friends erupt in laughter, it's true,
My aim's as bad as my morning brew.

I cook a meal meant to impress,
But burn the toast, now what a mess!
A fine soufflé? It plummets down,
Saved by the humor, not the crown.

I tried to dance, but stepped on toes,
In my own rhythm, how it goes!
A shuffle, a spin, then a fall,
Yet the joy of the moment enthralls.

Each blunder's a brushstroke on life's page,
Crafting a masterpiece, turning the stage.
With every misstep, we find our spark,
In this art of chaos, we leave a mark.

Juggling with Jokes

I tossed a joke, it hit the floor,
But laughter spring, oh what a roar!
Three balls in the air, oh what a sight,
One slipped away into the night.

A punchline flies, but ducks away,
"Did you hear?" I beg to say.
But then I trip, the joke's on me,
My circus act unveiled for free!

A clown's bright nose and floppy shoes,
I juggle words, with theatrical blues.
But when I miss, my face goes red,
For every quip left unsaid.

Yet laughter rings when chaos reigns,
Each blunder brings delightful gains.
We stumble forth, just join the fun,
In this juggling game, we've all won!

The Accidental Poet

With pen in hand, I scribble a thought,
Words tumble out, but wait, I'm caught!
Each line appears, a twist in rhyme,
Accidental art, just wasting time.

My quill takes flight, then lands with a flop,
Verses that soar, then simply drop.
I try for depth, yet wind up light,
In this whimsical space, I take flight.

But poems twist like my tangled hair,
Each stanza's a joke, laid out with flair.
My heart spills ink with a wobbly pen,
In laughter's embrace, I start again.

So here's to the slip, to words gone astray,
In the grand comedy that leads the way.
For poetry blooms where humor brews,
In the accidental, we've nothing to lose!

The Fractured Fairy Tale

Once upon a time in a land so grand,
a princess lost her shoe in the shifting sand.
A frog in a tux, with a wink and a grin,
took a leap to romance, chaos to begin.

The wicked queen slipped on her own magic spell,
as the knight chased a squirrel, oh what the hell!
Each turn was a chuckle, a giggle, a blunder,
as dragons tripped over the clouds in thunder.

With a flip and a flop, the story unwinded,
a dance with the jester, the court was reminded.
That happy endings sometimes are bumpy,
and the view from the bubbles can get quite lumpy.

In this fractured tale, where mishaps abound,
a joyful laughter is all that we found.
For in every stumble, a lesson we see,
in the silliest moments, we truly are free.

Where Accidents Spark Magic

In a world where mishaps bring giggles and cheer,
a broomstick went sideways, oh dear, oh dear!
A wizard with potions slipped on a floor,
a rainbow exploded, what fun was in store!

The mirror had trouble reflecting the truth,
a reflection of chaos, a sight of lost youth.
A lizard in glasses gave wisecracks galore,
making spells that just simply ignited a roar!

With each spell gone wrong, new wonders arose,
as gardens grew cupcakes, oh what a prose!
The sun wore a hat, while shadows would dance,
accidents turned magic, a wondrous romance!

And as giggles echoed, the moon winked down,
while fairies played pranks on a sleepy old town.
In every mishap, a twinkle can start,
where accidents linger, you'll find joy at heart.

A Compendium of Clumsy Steps

In a grand ballroom where everyone strolled,
a tap dance went bust, as a mishap unfolds.
With a trip and a tumble, a slip on the floor,
a pirouetting waiter ran straight for the door.

With a flurry of laughter, the crowd did unite,
as the chandeliers swayed with delight in the night.
An elegant spin turned a cringe into glee,
ostrich feathers flew like a whimsical spree!

A jester on stilts tried to offer a toast,
but lost in the crowd, he became quite the ghost.
With feet that were tangled and hats flying high,
we danced through the night, oh my, oh my!

In this compendium of blunders we find,
a rhythm of joy that's one of a kind.
For with every misstep, the laughter it grows,
in the hearts of the clumsy, pure magic bestows.

The Lighthearted Labyrinth

In the twists and the turns of a maze made of fun,
every corner held giggles, laughter on the run.
A minotaur danced with a twirl and a spin,
but tripped on his tail and fell right in!

A clever young maiden with shoes made of cheese,
slipped right through the entrance with comical ease.
Each path held a jest, each hedge a surprise,
and winks from the owls who peeked with wise eyes.

Beneath the bright lanterns, shadows would play,
as jesters in motion would lead us astray.
But following laughter, we'd find our way out,
with humor as guide, banishing doubt.

In this lighthearted labyrinth, fun is the key,
a place where we flourish, so wild and so free.
For every dead-end brings a chuckle and tune,
and joy fills the air like a bright afternoon.

The Jester's Misstep

In shoes too big, he danced around,
Tripping over all he found.
A pie in face, a slip on floor,
The crowd erupts, they beg for more.

His hat askew, the bells all jingle,
He juggles fruit, but they all tingle.
An orange flies, it hits a clown,
Laughter spills, as he falls down.

With painted grin, he tries to sing,
But every note's a silly thing.
A custard splash, a wig askew,
He bows and laughs, the world is true.

Yet in his folly, wisdom hides,
A chuckle shared, the joy abides.
With every jest, he finds a friend,
In every spill, a giggle bends.

Whims of the Wayward

A squirrel steals his shiny shoe,
He runs in circles, what to do?
The world just spins, a dizzy dance,
As he stumbles, seizes chance.

With mismatched socks and upside-down,
He greets the day, a merry clown.
A pie on porch, a splash of cream,
He laughs aloud, it's all a dream.

Each wrong turn leads to a surprise,
A cantaloupe beneath the skies.
He finds a duck, it quacks so bright,
Together they prance, what a sight!

In every folly, laughter's found,
The jester's heart, no bounds around.
So leave your roadmaps on the shelf,
Embrace the whim, just be yourself.

Laughter in the Fall

The leaves are falling, colors bright,
He trips and tumbles, what a sight!
A pumpkin rolls, he chases fast,
   Into a puddle, sail he casts.

The children giggle, gather 'round,
As he twists and turns, falls on ground.
A whistle blows, a kite takes flight,
   As he watches, mischief ignites.

With every gust, his hat takes wing,
He runs to catch it, what a fling!
A dog barks loud, joins in the fun,
Chasing shadows, they quickly run.

For in the blunders, joy is found,
He spins and dances, lost but proud.
Embrace the stumble, let it roll,
In every fall, you'll find your soul.

Serendipitous Follies

A coffee spill upon his shirt,
He laughs it off, the day's absurd.
His sandwich flies, a bird's delight,
As he waves hello, what a sight!

In crooked ties and mismatched shoes,
He struts about in vibrant hues.
A tumble here, a slip right there,
With every blunder, he sheds a care.

A pair of socks, one striped, one plain,
He grins and twirls in playful rain.
With every whisper of the breeze,
A chuckle bursts, his heart's at ease.

So here's to folly, here's to cheer,
Embrace the dance, let smiles appear.
For in the chaos, joys await,
Laugh with abandon; it's never late.

www.ingramcontent.com/pod-product-compliance
Lightning Source LLC
Chambersburg PA
CBHW051643160426
43209CB00004B/778